DRUGS **the facts about**
STEROIDS

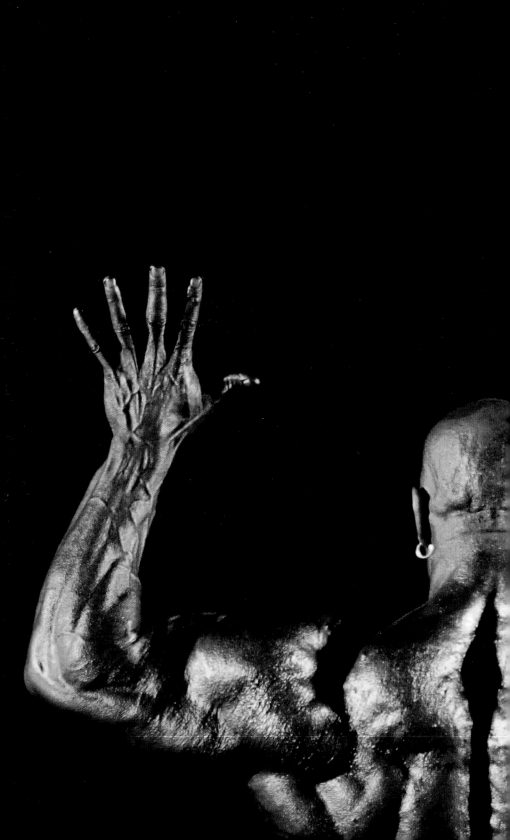

DRUGS the facts about
STEROIDS

Suzanne LeVert

Benchmark Books

Series Consultant: Dr. Amy Kohn, Chief Executive Officer, YWCA of White Plains and Central Westchester, New York. Thanks to John M. Roll, PhD, Director of Behavioral Pharmacology at UCLA Integrated Substance Abuse Programs, for his expert reading of this manuscript.

Benchmark Books
Marshall Cavendish
99 White Plains Road
Tarrytown, NY 10591-9001
www.marshallcavendish.us

All Internet sites were available and accurate when sent to press.

Library of Congress Cataloging-in-Publication Data

Levert, Suzanne.
The facts about steroids / Suzanne Levert.
p. cm. — (Drugs)
Includes bibliographical references and index.
ISBN 0-7614-1808-3
1. Anabolic steroids—Juvenile literature. 2. Doping in sports
—Juvenile literature. I. Title. II. Series: Drugs (Benchmark Books (Firm))

RC1230.L48 2008
362.29'9—dc22
2004011852

Photo research by Joan Meisel

Cover photo: Scott Barbour/Getty Images

Photo credits: *Corbis:* San Francisco Chronicle/San Francisco Chronicle, 6; Bettmann, 9, 33; Kevin lamarque/Reuters, 50; Reuters, 60; ML Sinibladi, 64; Pete Saloutos, 72; Rob Lewine, 72. *Getty:* Scott Barbour, 1, 2-3, 4-5, 79; David McNew, 18; Karen Levy/Allsport, 27; Nick Laham/Allsport, 55. *Photo Researchers, Inc.:* John M. Daugherty, 22; Michael Abbey, 24; John Bavosi, 43.

Printed in China
3 5 6 4 2

CONTENTS

MAJOR LEAGUE BASEBALL PLAYER BARRY BONDS WITH HIS PERSONAL TRAINER, GREG ANDERSON. IN FEBRUARY 2004 ANDERSON WAS CHARGED WITH DISTRIBUTING ILLEGAL STEROIDS TO PROFESSIONAL ATHLETES. AT THE TIME OF THE INDICTMENT, U.S. ATTORNEY GENERAL JOHN ASHCROFT SAID "STEROIDS ARE BAD FOR SPORTS, THEY'RE BAD FOR PLAYERS, THEY'RE BAD FOR YOUNG PEOPLE WHO HOLD ATHLETES UP AS ROLE MODELS."

1 The Game of Steroids

"THE USE OF performance-enhancing drugs like steroids in baseball, football, and other sports is dangerous," stated President George W. Bush. "And it sends the wrong message: that there are shortcuts to accomplishment, and that performance is more important than character. So tonight I call on team owners, union representatives, coaches, and players to take the lead, to send the right signal, to get tough, and to get rid of steroids now."

President Bush made that statement in his State of the Union address on January 20, 2004. His comments reflected a growing problem in amateur and professional athletics: the illegal use of steroids. In February 2004, the controversy grew when a grand jury in San Francisco, California indicted four men who were accused of distributing steroids to professional athletes. One of the accused was Greg Anderson, personal trainer to baseball star Barry Bonds. At the time, Bonds held the record for most home runs in a single season. The others facing charges were two executives of BALCO Labs nutritional supplement company, and a track coach.

Indeed, steroid use among professional athletes appears to be entrenched. The National Football League spends about $10 million a year on steroid and drug programs. According to a March 3, 2004 article in the *New York Times,* drug testing showed positive results for 5 to 7 percent of professional baseball players in 2003. A result of these findings is mandatory steroid testing of all major league baseball players.

"It's no secret what's going on in baseball. At least half the guys are using steroids," Ken Caminiti, the National Baseball League's Most Valuable Player in 1996, told a reporter from *Sports Illustrated* in May 2002. "They talk about it. They joke about it with each other. . . . I don't want to hurt teammates or friends. But I've got nothing to hide."

The scandal provoked by Caminiti's observations of steroid use was hardly the first to hit the sports world. In 1988 Canadian sprinter Ben Johnson lost his gold medal at the Summer Olympics when, after running the 100-meter dash in 9.79 seconds, he tested positive for a steroid called stanozolol. Forced to give up his medal—which went to the man in second place, American Carl Lewis—Johnson was also denied the right to run international races for two years.

CANADIAN SPRINTER BEN JOHNSON SET A WORLD RECORD FOR THE 100-METER DASH AT THE 1988 OLYMPICS. BUT AFTER TESTING POSITIVE FOR THE ANABOLIC STEROID STANOZOLOL HE WAS STRIPPED OF HIS GOLD MEDAL AND BANNED FROM COMPETING FOR TWO YEARS. JOHNSON TESTED POSITIVE AGAIN IN 1993 AND WAS BANNED FROM COMPETITION FOR LIFE.

The International Olympics Committee banned steroid use in 1975, and routine testing for steroids at the Olympic Games began about that time as well. In 1984 a random test of dozens of Olympic athletes revealed that more than half of those tested had taken steroids. This result showed a far higher percentage of athletes taking steroids than the first round of testing at the 1976 Olympics, which showed that just two percent of athletes had steroids in their systems.

What Is a Steroid?

A steroid is a hormonelike substance produced by the body. A hormone is a chemical messenger that directs body tissues and organs to act in certain ways. Steroids are substances closely related to the prime male hormone, testosterone. Testosterone is one of the main factors determining the development of secondary male characteristics, such as facial hair, deepening of the voice, and larger muscle size. However, women too produce small amounts of testosterone, and men produce small amounts of the prime female hormone, estrogen.

There are two different kinds of steroids: catabolic steroids and anabolic steroids. Catabolic steroids are those prescribed by physicians to reduce swelling, fever, and other symptoms of inflammation. Anabolic steroids are substances related to testosterone, the male sex hormone. They act on muscle tissue to build upon it and make it stronger. In fact, the word *anabolic* comes from a Greek word meaning "to build up."

It is important to note that anabolic steroids were originally developed and continue to be used for legitimate medical purposes. Researchers developed these substances in the 1930s primarily to treat a condition called hypogonadism. This condition exists when a man's body fails to produce enough testosterone for normal growth, development, and sexual function.

By performing experiments and studies about hypogonadism, scientists discovered that testosterone, which is a natural anabolic steroid, also worked directly on skeletal muscle, the muscle tissue that allows movement of the limbs. The knowledge and understanding they acquired led to the development of synthetic anabolic steroids. These drugs have legitimate medical purposes, such as the treatment of osteoporosis (thinning of bones) and immune system diseases like HIV, the virus that causes AIDS. But anabolic steroids are also used—illegally—by bodybuilders and weightlifters and by athletes in other sports, often with unhealthy, even deadly, results.

The marketing and sale of anabolic steroids is a multi-billion-dollar business in the United States and around the world—but an illegal business fraught with potentially severe legal penalties. Many countries, including the United States, have strict laws restricting the manufacture and sale of anabolic steroids. These laws and their enforcement have led to an underground black market industry.

The Problems with Steroids
The good news is that legal prescription and non-prescription medications derived from catabolic steroids can help to heal and strengthen the human body. The bad news is the damage caused to organs

11

and systems by the illegal use of unregulated anabolic steroids and related supplements.

Study after study proves that the excessive use of anabolic steroids leads to unwanted and often dangerous side effects. The chart below lists the effects that using illegal steroids may have on the young men and women who take them.

In addition to physical side effects—which include lowered sperm count, enlarged breasts, and decreased testicle size in men and disruptions in menstruation, increased facial hair, and decreased breast size in women—steroid use can trigger psychological and emotional side effects as well. These side effects may include mood swings, aggression, depression (especially upon stopping the use of steroids), and even violent or suicidal behavior.

STEROID-RELATED PROBLEMS

IN MALES	IN FEMALES	IN BOTH MALES AND FEMALES
Sterility	Irreversible hair loss	Acne
Larger breasts	Changes in or cessation of menstrual cycle	Irreversible hair loss
Increased rate of testicular and prostate cancer		Bladder problems
	Smaller breasts	
Decreased testicle size	More facial and body hair	Rapid weight gain or loss

The illegal use of steroids by athletes—professional and amateur alike—represents a serious social problem. Athletes who buy and use these drugs without a prescription are not only breaking the law but are also cheating. They are attempting to win the easy way, by gaining an advantage over opponents through increasing their muscle mass and strength with substances banned by virtually all amateur and professional sports organizations. Just as steroids pose risks to the health of the individuals who use them, they also undermine the integrity of athletics for fans of all ages.

Why Take Steroids?
With these well-known dangers associated with steroid use, why would people, particularly young people, risk their health by using them. Just open a fitness or fashion magazine or turn on the television during prime time to see what motivates some people to take steroids. The drive to look rail-thin like fashion models or rippled with muscles like bodybuilders is strong in our society, especially among young people. The health and fitness industry is a multi-billion-dollar one, and millions of people struggle to look like the often unrealistic images publicized in the media.

Indeed, although most people who take steroids do so in order to improve their athletic performance, not all steroid users wish to increase their prowess on the playing field. Other people, particularly young women, take steroids in order to

Joe M. is a sixteen-year-old high school junior. Joe always assumed he'd be made captain of his football team in his senior year. He dreamed of obtaining a football scholarship after that, and maybe even playing on a professional team.

But Joe's career as an athlete was cut short for a number of reasons, all having to do with his use of illegal steroids—substances he used to build up his strength in order to make the team and perform well.

I bought my first steroids, called Anadrol, from the brother of a friend of mine when I was a freshman. Almost as soon as I started taking them, I saw results—my arms got so solid, my leg muscles were like iron. I could run faster and take harder hits than ever before. I felt great.

But after taking them for a while, my personality started to change, I guess. I didn't feel it, really, but my girlfriend and even the guys on my team sure did. I got aggressive with her, I started fighting with my teammates, my coach started benching me because I was out of control. My dad came to me and asked me what was wrong. I didn't think anything was wrong, but my life was falling apart around me.

At the beginning of his junior year, however, Joe's school instituted a new random drug-testing program.

The very first week, I was caught. I gave them a urine sample that I knew was dirty [containing evidence of steroid use], but there was nothing I could do. Two weeks later, the coach called my dad, my dad came to school, and I was off the team. I know I'm still young, but I feel like I've ruined my life—all to get muscled up.

decrease their body fat levels more quickly than they could by improving their diets and increasing their exercise levels. Because anabolic steroids can help to decrease body fat, young women often use them on their quest to achieve the "perfect body" they see in magazines, televisions programs, and movies.

Today, nearly as many men as women say they are unhappy with the way they look. According to the *British Medical Journal,* the number of men who openly report dissatisfaction with their physical appearance has tripled. According to an article by Sid Kirchheimer of *Web MD Medical News,* therapists report seeing 50 percent more men for evaluation and treatment of eating disorders today than they did in the 1990s. In fact, eating disorders, including bulimia and anorexia nervosa, are on the rise among athletes and nonathletes, men and women, alike. Athletes competing in sports such as gymnastics, running, wrestling, and crew are particularly at risk.

For some people, particularly adolescents, the abuse of steroids is merely part of a pattern of high-risk behaviors that may also include drinking and driving, failing to wear seat belts, and abusing other illicit drugs.

Who Takes Steroids?
Although competitive athletes using steroids make the most news, they are far from the only people who use and abuse anabolic steroids. Males and females, rich and poor, blacks, whites, Asians, Hispanics—steroid use and abuse occurs among

members of all economic classes and racial groups.

The fact that young people take steroids is particularly alarming. One study of children between the ages of nine and twelve found that nearly 3 percent of those surveyed had used steroids. Although research suggests that steroid abuse among adolescents may have leveled off, it still remains at alarming rates. The Monitoring the Future Study, funded by the National Institute on Drug Abuse, surveys drug abuse among adolescents in middle schools and high schools across the United States. The 2002 study found that more than 1.7 percent of eighth and tenth graders and 2.7 percent of twelfth graders had taken anabolic steroids at least once in their lives. A study commissioned by Blue Cross and Blue Shield in 2001 estimated that at least one million young people from twelve to seventeen years of age have taken steroids or other performance-enhancing substances at some time in their lives.

Here are some other statistics to consider:

• According to a 1996 report by the Drug Enforcement Administration (DEA), between 5 and 15 percent of male high school students and one percent of female students have used steroids at least once by the time they are seniors.

• Male steroid users outnumber female users by more than three to one, although the number of female users continue to grow.

16

In a survey published by the news magazine *U.S. News & World Report* in 1992, 57 percent of teens who use steroids said that reading so-called muscle magazines influenced them to do so. The fact that they believed that famous athletes used steroids influenced 42 percent of teen users to take the drugs.

And teens from the United States are not the only ones using these substances. In a survey of British fourteen- to fifteen-year-olds conducted by researchers at the University of Essex in 2000, steroids were found to be the third most commonly used drug following amphetamines and marijuana, with more than 2 percent of the teenage boys questioned admitting they had used them.

Although little data exists on the extent of steroid abuse by adults, experts estimate that hundreds of thousands of people aged eighteen and older abuse anabolic steroids annually. The use and abuse of illegal steroids is a problem throughout the United States and a problem that grows every year.

LAUREN POWERS POSES AT THE ANNUAL VENICE CLASSIC BODYBUILDING COMPETITION. VENICE BEACH, WHICH IS IN SOUTHERN CALIFORNIA, IS ALSO KNOWN AS MUSCLE BEACH.

2 Steroids and the Body

WHILE BOTH MEN and **women produce** testosterone naturally, women do so in much smaller quantities. Men make about 2.5 to 11 milligrams of testosterone every day, while women produce just a tenth of that amount. Anabolic steroids are synthetic forms of testosterone produced in laboratories by scientists and technicians. People who take anabolic steroids to try to build muscle typically take about 100 milligrams of these substances per day, which is well over ten times the amount they would produce naturally.

What Are the Natural Steroids?

There are three basic types of steroids found naturally in the body: corticosteroids, the female hormones estrogen and progesterone, and male hormones such as testosterone. Corticosteroids are natural or synthetic hormones. Natural corticosteroids are produced by the gland called the adrenal cortex, which influences or controls such body activities as carbohydrate and protein metabolism, electrolyte and water balance, and the functioning of the cardiovascular system, the skeletal muscles, the kidneys, and other organs. When used as medicine, these steroids are found in prescription and nonprescription creams and ointments that control rashes and itching.

The female sex hormones, estrogen and progesterone, are responsible for the development of secondary sex characteristics in women. They also maintain the female reproductive system. Estrogen and progesterone are the active ingredients in birth control tablets and hormone replacement therapy.

The male sex hormones are called androgens. The prime androgen is testosterone, which is responsible for the development of male secondary sex characteristics and the male reproductive system. Doctors commonly prescribe synthetic or natural testosterone to treat female breast cancer and androgen deficiency in men, and to stimulate growth, weight gain, and red blood cell production for people suffering from certain cancers and other conditions. In addition to building bone and muscle, testosterone

- maintains sexual organs and function
- triggers hair growth, especially on the face, and
- influences emotions.

Androgens, including testosterone, are also used to create anabolic steroids—drugs designed specifically to grow muscle tissue. More than a hundred different anabolic steroids have been developed, but all of them require a prescription to be purchased legally in the United States.

The Muscle Machine

There are more than 650 individual muscles in the human body. Muscles make up about 40 percent of a man's weight and 23 percent of a woman's. There are three different kinds of muscle tissue. Each kind serves a different purpose and works in a different way.

Cardiac muscle, for instance, is found only in the heart. It is controlled by an internal electrical signal, called a pacemaker, that causes it to contract about once a second every minute of life. Another kind of muscle is smooth muscle. It is found throughout the body, including in the intestines, bladder, and uterus. Signals from the body's central nervous system trigger smooth muscle to contract.

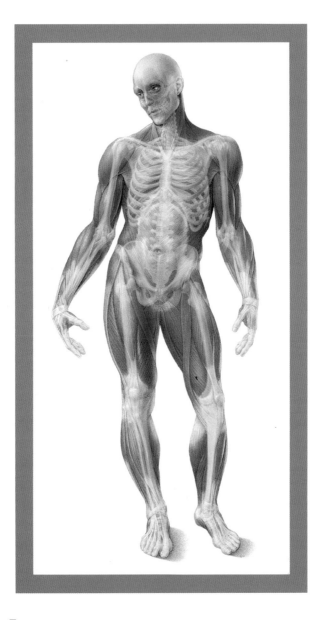

THIS MEDICAL ILLUSTRATION SHOWS THE PLACEMENT AND CONNECTION OF SKELETAL MUSCLE TO BONE. THE HUMAN BODY CONTAINS OVER SIX HUNDRED ACTIVE MUSCLES.

Skeletal muscle, also known as striated or voluntary muscle, is the most abundant of the three types of muscle in the human body. As its name implies, skeletal, or voluntary, muscle is muscle that one can control. It moves the limbs, fingers and toes, and face. For instance, holding this book calls on actions of voluntary muscle, and the brain signals certain muscles to move the eyes across the page.

The makeup of skeletal muscles allows them to contract and release, and thus move. Inside skeletal muscle tissue is a bundle of cablelike tissue called fibers. Each of those fibers contains still smaller fibers called fibrils. In a long muscle, such as those in the legs, a single fibril can be up to one foot long and as thin as a human hair. Fibrils are made up of two types of proteins: actin and myosin.

Most skeletal muscles are arranged in pairs, with each muscle in the pair performing an opposite movement. For example, to move a leg, actin strands slide past myosin strands, making the muscle contract. When the actin strands in the leg slide in the other direction, the muscle relaxes, returning the leg to its original position.

How Do Muscles Grow and Become Stronger?
The use of hormones and other substances to enhance strength and virility is centuries old. Long before modern medical science identified testosterone as a source of strength, humans associated prowess with the male sex organs. Charles E. Yesalis and Virginia S. Cowart, authors of *The*

Steroids Game, tell of a healer in India who even advocated eating testicle tissue as a cure for impotence way back in 140 B.C.E. It turns out that this medical lore contains much more scientific truth than one might guess. Testosterone actually works to stimulate the tissue-building process, thus helping to make muscle stronger; so it is after all a "source of strength."

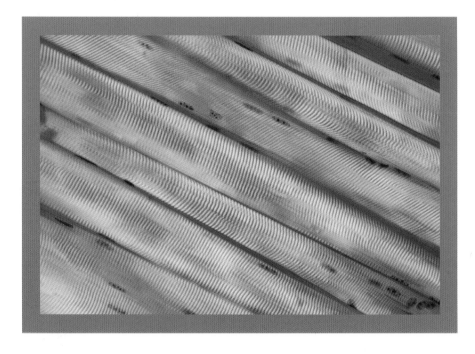

STRIATED MUSCLE FIBERS, SHOWN HERE MAGNIFIED **106** TIMES, ARE WHAT MAKE UP VOLUNTARY MUSCLE, THE MOST ABUNDANT OF THE THREE TYPES OF MUSCLE IN THE HUMAN BODY.

Like all hormones, testosterone is a chemical messenger. In the case of muscle building, testosterone triggers muscle cells to produce specific proteins from raw materials and those proteins cause muscle tissue mass to increase. Other messages testosterone sends to body cells result in the development of different masculine characteristics, such as the deepening of the voice, growth of facial hair, and a decrease in body fat. These characteristics develop naturally when a male hits puberty and his body begins to produce testosterone in sufficient quantities. They can also develop or be augmented when males take the synthetic forms of testosterone, commonly known as anabolic steroids, in order to speed up and enhance their ability to develop strong and big muscles.

Steroid Use and Abuse

Experts believe that more than one million Americans have abused illegal anabolic steroids. Three hundred thousand Americans do so every year, and from 2 to 10 percent of those abusers are teenagers. Steroid abusers have many sources from which to buy these substances, from the Internet and mail-order companies to street pushers and corrupt physicians.

How Do You Take Anabolic Steroids?

People take anabolic steroids in one of four ways: by mouth, by injection, through nasal sprays, and by skin cream or patches. In all forms, these steroids have had their chemical structures altered to enable them to be metabolized by the body, either to slow down their entry into the bloodstream (in the case of intramuscular injections) or to slow down their removal from the body in order to protect the liver (in the case of steroids taken in pill form).

There are dozens of brands of steroids and related products. The chart below lists some of the most common and popular.

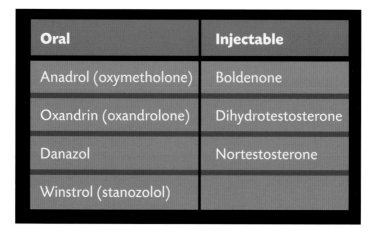

Oral	Injectable
Anadrol (oxymetholone)	Boldenone
Oxandrin (oxandrolone)	Dihydrotestosterone
Danazol	Nortestosterone
Winstrol (stanozolol)	

What Is a Steroid Cycle?

Most people take steroids in a particular order and for a particular amount of time, called a cycle. Each cycle lasts from six to twelve weeks or more. In an attempt to further enhance the way steroids work, some abusers try either or both of these two methods of use:

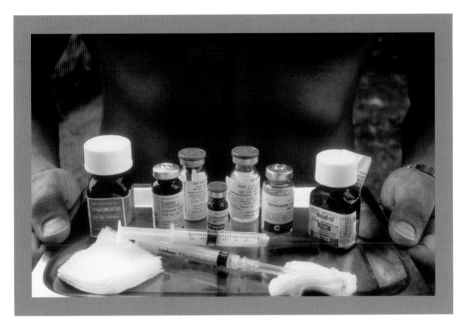

STEROIDS CAN BE TAKEN BY INJECTION, BY MOUTH, THROUGH NASAL SPRAYS, AND BY SKIN CREAM OR PATCHES.

Stacking. Abusers frequently take two or more anabolic steroids together, mixing oral and/or injectable types, sometimes adding drugs such as stimulants or painkillers. The rationale for stacking is a belief, as yet unproven, that the different drugs interact to produce a greater effect on muscle size than could be obtained by simply increasing the dose of a single drug. It also decreases the likelihood that the user will develop a tolerance to one type of steroid.

Like most people who take steroids, Jason, a sixteen-year-old junior, started out by taking the drugs in pill form.

> That wasn't so bad. I could stand taking pills. And it didn't make me feel like an addict or a drug abuser. But then someone convinced me that I'd get better and faster results if I injected the drugs. So that's what I did. The first time I did it, I almost fainted—the needle was almost two inches long!

In addition to the discomfort of injecting drugs, steroid abusers also run the risk of spreading infections such as HIV (the virus that causes AIDS) if they choose to share needles. Jason recounts,

> I was always really careful, and so were my friends. But we knew people down at the gym who didn't take the trouble or spend the money to get their own needles and syringes. I worry about them all the time, wondering if anyone ever got sick.

Jason stopped taking steroids during the summer before his junior year, after he heard that his school would be instituting a random drug-testing program.

It wasn't just that I was afraid of getting caught. I was starting to think the side effects weren't worth it: my skin was breaking out bad, and my moods were pretty unpredictable too. I tapered off during the summer and I don't think I'll ever touch them again.

Pyramiding. Using this technique, a steroid abuser begins by using low doses of a substance and then gradually increases the doses for six to twelve weeks. In the second half of the cycle, he or she slowly decreases the doses to zero. In some cases, a second cycle follows, during which the person continues to train with weights but doesn't take steroids. Abusers believe that pyramiding allows the body time to adjust to the high doses, and the drug-free cycle allows time for the body's hormonal system to recuperate. As with stacking, the perceived benefits of pyramiding have not been proven by any scientific testing.

What Other Muscle-building Substances Do People Take?

In addition to anabolic steroids, there are several other substances that some people use in an effort to improve their athletic performance and body shape. Falling under the general heading of dietary supplements, these substances are largely unregulated by any government agency—such as the federal Food and Drug Administration (FDA), which regulates such legitimate products as prescription and over-the-counter drugs. As a result, manufacturers of dietary supplements do not have to prove that the substances are safe or effective.

Knowledge about these supplements grew by leaps and bounds in 1998, when reporters revealed that baseball player Mark McGwire used the sup-

Stacy was thirteen when she started to worry about her weight and body image, and she was fifteen when she started taking steroids. It took her four years, but she finally kicked her steroid habit. Now twenty-two and graduating from college, she looks back on her high school years with a bit of sadness and regret.

I hated the way I looked when I was in high school. Hated it. I felt pudgy and dumpy, even though I was at a normal weight for my body type. No matter how much I worked out, I didn't look like the models I saw on TV or even the cheerleaders at my school. My friend's brother, a college football player, started me on steroids. I took Danazol [an oral steroid] mostly—I never used needles. It worked for a while. I did change the shape of my body. But the price was too high. My breasts practically disappeared, I had awful mood swings, and worst of all, I had to hide a huge part of my life from my family and friends. I didn't have to worry about getting caught—my friend gave me the steroids and my school didn't have random drug-testing—but I felt awful about it, all the time. I felt like I was a fake.

posed muscle-building substances androstenedione and creatine during his successful bid to break Roger Maris's home run record. McGwire's powerful swing and rippling biceps were the focus of attention as he hit seventy home runs that year—just enough to beat out Chicago Cub Sammy Sosa, who reportedly used creatine himself, for the new record. Could his use of supplements have been what made the difference? Did he cheat by doing so? Since major league baseball did not ban these substances at that time, he did nothing legally wrong. But questions remain about the ethical implications—to say nothing of the long-term medical effects—of using muscle-enhancing, energy-boosting supplements.

Nevertheless, according to the *Nutrition Business Journal,* which provides market research for the dietary supplement industry, U.S. sales of pills, powders, bars, and beverages promoted to boost athletic performance reached $1.26 billion in 1997 and continues to grow.

The two most popular supplements are:

Androstenedione (also known as Andro): East German researchers developed this substance in the 1970s in an attempt to boost the performance of Olympic swimmers and other athletes. Andro was introduced commercially in the United States in the mid-1990s. Marketers widely claim that a 100-

AT THE 1976 OLYMPICS IN MONTREAL, THE EAST GERMAN SWIM TEAM WON
ELEVEN OUT OF THIRTEEN TITLES. THE WOMEN'S RELAY TEAM IS SHOWN HERE
WITH KORNELIA ENDER (FAR RIGHT) WHO TOOK FOUR GOLD MEDALS AND ONE
SILVER. ENDER LATER REVEALED THAT SHE STARTED RECEIVING STEROID INJECTIONS
AT THE AGE OF THIRTEEN.

milligram dose of androstenedione increases the male hormone testosterone by up to 300 percent. The increase, according to marketers, lasts for about three hours. The Association of Professional Team Physicians, composed of team doctors from professional sports teams, has recommended that androstenedione be banned from all competitive sports. According to the group, Andro has a chemical structure like that of an anabolic steroid. The governing bodies of virtually all competitive sports ban anabolic steroids, in part because of their health risks and in part because the government has little regulatory power over their content and effectiveness.

Creatine: Creatine is a combination of three amino acids (building blocks of protein) that occur naturally in the body, are contained in meats, and are eliminated in your urine. The extent of the use of creatine remains unknown, but a Mayo Clinic study showed that more than 8 percent of 328 high school athletes used creatine at some point in their lives. Creatine monohydrate is a compound produced by the body that helps release energy in muscles, and some research indicates that it may help provide short bursts of energy to those who take it. Muscle cramps and nausea are typical short-term side effects, but no studies have been performed on possible long-term effects of using the substance.

Whether professional and amateur athletes will continue to use these and other largely unregulated supplements, and the long-term physical and psychological effects on all those who take them, remains to be seen. In the meantime, research continues to show that taking anabolic steroids and certain supplements poses serious medical risks.

3 The Health Risks

STEROIDS ARE HORMONES, chemical triggers of body actions and reactions. Virtually every bodily process, from sleep to digestion to memory, is launched and carried out with help from these substances. Anabolic steroids mimic the bodybuilding effects of the male hormone testosterone. Their most direct effect is on muscle tissue, helping the body to more efficiently synthesize and metabolize the protein that muscles need to grow and strengthen. Most people who use steroids report an increase in muscle mass, strength, and endurance that they believe would not have occurred as quickly— or maybe at all—without the steroids.

But steroids also have wide-ranging effects on other bodily organs and processes, and not all of these effects are healthy, especially over the long term.

Physical Effects and Side Effects

Every cell in the body—not just muscle cells—metabolizes, or break down, anabolic steroids. The major systems and organs most likely to be affected by the action of anabolic steroids are the liver, the nervous system, the cardiovascular system, the sex organs, and the immune system.

It should be noted at the outset that not everyone is affected by steroids in the same way. Indeed, the effects and side effects of taking steroids vary widely from individual to individual.

The Liver: The liver is the largest gland in the human body and one of the most complex of all human organs. It serves as the body's main chemical factory and is one of its major storehouses of food. The liver is one of the organs responsible for eliminating toxins and waste from the body. As such, it is responsible for clearing the body of drugs, including anabolic steroids. Since steroid doses are usually so high, the liver must strain to try to keep up. This strain leaves the liver vulnerable to the development of cysts, which are sacs of fluid, and perhaps cancerous tumors.

The Kidneys: Like the liver, the kidneys also help to clean the body of wastes. They produce urine, a clear fluid full of waste products. Urine is stored in the bladder until eliminated through urination. In rare cases, anabolic steroids can damage the kidneys.

The Cardiovascular System: The cardiovascular system consists of the heart and the blood vessels, which bring blood containing oxygen and vital nutrients to every cell in the body. Anabolic steroids affect this system in many ways. Steroid users frequently have high levels of harmful cholesterol, which can block the arteries around the heart. Such blockages can cause a heart attack, which occurs when the heart does not receive enough oxygen. High cholesterol also causes traveling blood clots that can damage other parts of the body. When a clot blocks blood from the brain, a condition called a stroke occurs. Finally, some animal studies show that anabolic steroids damage the heart muscle itself, causing a disease called cardiomyopathy. Cardiomyopathy is a progressive disease in which the heart muscle becomes weaker and larger and thus unable to act as a pump to push blood through the body. And taking steroids raises blood pressure, which is the amount of force required for the heart and blood vessels to move the blood through the body. High blood pressure can result in several serious health problems, including higher risk of heart attacks and strokes.

The Immune System: The immune system is the body's main line of defense against germs and other disease-causing substances. It consists of several glands in the body that produce disease-fighting cells. Some studies show that steroids suppress the body's immune system, which leads to an increased vulnerability to infection and disease, even to the development of cancer.

The Reproductive System: In both men and women the use of steroids affects the reproductive system. Anabolic steroids resemble testosterone, the prime male hormone. When women take testosterone, it counteracts the feminizing effects of estrogen, the prime female hormone. That imbalance causes side effects such as the loss of scalp hair, growth of facial hair, and deepening of the voice. In addition, steroids may alter the menstrual cycle, often shortening it or causing it to stop altogether. Although this effect may be reversed once steroid use ceases, women may not be able to become pregnant while taking steroids. Most men who take high doses of steroids become infertile while they use the drug. They also develop some feminine characteristics, such as the loss of body hair, decreased size of testicles, and increased breast size. While some of these effects are reversible, some are not.

"The truth is, I started taking steroids to lose weight and to get more fit," admits Katy, a fifteen-year-old high school sophomore. Like most kids her age, Katy was just starting to date and wanted to be more attractive to the boys in her class.

> But everything backfired. My breasts became smaller—which isn't good!—and I started growing lots more hair on my face, which isn't exactly cute. Worse than that, after about six months my period stopped and I started feeling weird, not myself.

Katy's mother is the one who began to notice the changes in her daughter.

> She's the one who confronted me. She thought I was using other kinds of drugs, like cocaine or something. And she'd noticed that my periods had stopped and so she thought I was pregnant. At first, she was really relieved that it was "only" steroids, and she made me stop. But when my withdrawal symptoms started—I was really sick, nauseated all the time, really irritable, and really craving more steroids—we both realized how serious it all was. We worked with a counselor and a doctor to wean me off the stuff. I'll never touch it again, that's for sure.

Musculoskeletal System: Bones begin to grow and develop even before one is born. They continue to do so through adolescence. When the concentration of sex hormones, including testosterone, reaches a certain level during adolescence, it triggers the body to slow down and then stop bone growth. In this way, abnormally high testosterone levels that occur with steroid abuse during adolescence may result in an abnormally small stature and stunted bone growth.

What Happens to the Rest of the Body?

Steroids affect the body in various, and often quite serious, ways. Listed here is a head-to-toe guide to steroid effects and side effects:

The Skull: Steroids may act to change the size of the skull because of their effects on bone metabolism. In adults, anabolic steroid abuse can cause growth in bone mass, while in children and adolescents it can stunt bone growth.

The Skin: Steroids cause the body to retain water, which raises blood pressure. High blood pressure can cause the skin to take on a reddish hue as veins and arteries close to the skin pump blood with more force. In other cases, the skin of steroid users may take on a yellowish tinge because of the effects of steroids on the liver. If the liver fails to function properly, it produces too much of a yellowish-colored substance called bilirubin. When too much bilirubin circulates in the body, a disease called jaundice occurs. Most people who take steroids also suffer from acne, a skin condition often triggered by hormonal imbalances.

The Shoulders and Arms: Athletes who use steroids tend to develop very strong upper body muscles called the deltoid, trapezius, and latissimus dorsi muscles. These muscles surround and support the shoulders. The biceps and triceps—the muscles in the upper arms—are also affected dramatically by steroid use. The lower body may remain normal-sized even as these muscles in the upper body grow.

The Chest: Other muscles that seem to be particularly susceptible to the effects of steroids are those in the chest, including the pectoral muscles.

The Breasts: The effects of extra testosterone—a male hormone—on the body are different in men and women. In men the use of anabolic steroids may cause breast tissue to increase, a condition called gynecomastia; while most women who take steroids find that their breast tissue tends to shrink.

The Abdominals: Steroids help reduce body fat even as they promote muscle growth. Some users of steroids find that their waists shrink while other areas of the body grow.

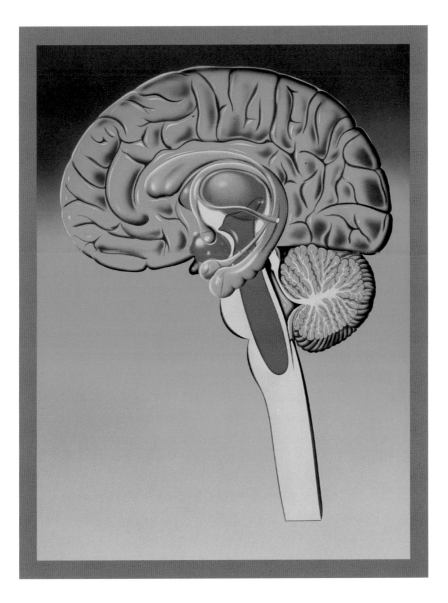

THE LIMBIC SYSTEM OF THE BRAIN, SHOWN HERE IN RED, PINK, AND ORANGE, CONTROLS EMOTION AND MEMORY.

The Testicles: The hormonal system is one that requires balance in order to function. When the level of one hormone shoots up, the body "knows" to stop making more of that hormone. Taking steroids, which resemble testosterone, causes the testicles to stop making its own. After a while, the testicles shrink and the body produces less sperm.

The Knees: Use of steroids may damage tendons and ligaments. Although research on humans on this topic is scarce, animal studies from the 1980s show that the damage to joints begins within a few days of steroid use and that exercise combined with steroid use makes it worse. The lab animals injected with steroids ended up with stiffer, weaker tendons, which were more easily damaged as muscle tissue grew stronger. In addition to the results of these animal studies, athletes who use steroids frequently complain that they suffer more often from pulled tendons and ligaments than those who don't use steroids.

The Psychological Effects and Side Effects of Steroid Use

The human brain and nervous system form a vast communications network, larger and more complicated than any digital cellular network. Every emotion felt, action taken, and physiological function undergone, is processed by the brain and the nerve fibers that extend down the spinal cord and throughout the body.

Moods, emotions, and memories primarily occur in a part of the brain called the limbic system, as well as another part of the brain called the cortex. The limbic system is a group of related nervous system structures located in the midbrain. Scientists believe that this highly complex region receives and regulates emotional information. It helps govern sexual desire, appetite, and stress. It does so by sending messages through the nervous system to various systems and cells of the body.

Brain chemicals called neurotransmitters—specifically serotonin, norepinephrine (also known as adrenalin), and dopamine—are among the body's chemicals that help to send messages through the nervous system. According to research, steroids disrupt the levels of these chemicals, and this disruption can lead to a variety of psychological and behaviorial changes. These changes include:

Mood Swings: Most people who take steroids say they experience feelings of excitement and exhilaration—at least for a while. But those feelings may soon disappear, only to be replaced by anger, sadness, and/or bad temper. Any time the levels of hormones in the body change, mood swings may result. Puberty, when young men and women are producing more sex hormones than ever before, is such a time. This is why teenagers are known for their moodiness, feeling energetic and optimistic one day and irritable or sad the next. Anabolic steroids disrupt hormone levels in the body, and thus may trigger extreme mood swings—especially in teenagers, whose bodies are already working hard to accommodate the natural hormonal changes that are occurring.

Sleep Disruption: Although for many teenagers getting sleep—and lots of it—comes quite naturally, sleep involves very complicated bodily processes. Like the processes that determine mood, they require proper hormonal balance. Teenagers and adults who take steroids often experience insomnia, the inability to fall or stay asleep.

Increased Aggression: Steroid experts Charles Yesalis and Virginia Cowart point out that the relationship between natural testosterone levels and aggressive behavior in animals is well documented. However, research has yet to make a direct and definite link between higher testosterone (or anabolic steroid) levels and aggressive or violent behavior. One recent study, conducted by a Northeastern University professor and published in a February 2003 issue of *Hormones and Behavior,* indicates that use of anabolic steroids may have long-term effects on behavior levels and aggression even after users stop taking the drugs. Nevertheless, anecdotal evidence of such increases in aggression have led to the term "'roid rage" to describe the anger and irritability many people who use steroids feel. In one 1983 survey, published in *The Physician and Sportsmedicine Online,* more than one half of male steroid users interviewed reported that steroids made them more irritable and aggressive. Accounts from women steroid users also indicate that taking steroids can cause hostile feelings. In 1985 the *Journal of the American Medical Association* published a study of ten women steroid users, eight of whom reported that they felt more aggressive—and trained harder—since using the drugs.

Impaired Judgment: The mood swings and other psychological disruptions caused by steroids may well contribute to the poor choices many steroid abusers make. These choices include the increased risk-taking behavior involved in buying and using the substances, which remain illegal.

Depression and Suicidal Behavior: People who take steroids often feel euphoric when they first take steroids. But many experience periods of feeling sad, even while still taking the drug. When people stop taking steroids altogether, however, they may

47

become clinically depressed. Depression is a disease involving an imbalance of neurotransmitters, particularly serotonin. Serotonin is involved in several physiological and psychological processes, including helping to regulate mood. Scientists believe that the use of anabolic steroids disrupts both the production of serotonin and the brain's ability to use it. When people stop taking steroids, the feelings of euphoria that those drugs may trigger cease and depression may develop. Although not all people who become depressed kill themselves, there is a direct link between serotonin levels, depression, and suicide. Suicide is among the leading causes of death in the United States and is among the three leading causes of death for those fifteen to thirty-four years of age. Although suicide is relatively rare among steroid users, scientists continue to study the links between the hormonal and neurotransmitter imbalances caused by steroids, the withdrawal symptoms caused by stopping steroid use, and depression and suicide among people who abuse or have abused steroids.

Other Substance Abuse Problems: Research also indicates that some users might turn to other drugs to alleviate some of the negative effects of anabolic steroids. For example, a study of 227 men admitted in 1999 to a private treatment center for dependence on heroin found that 9.3 percent had abused anabolic steroids before trying any other illicit drug. Of these 9.3 percent, 86 percent (eighteen people) first used heroin to counteract insomnia and irritability resulting from the anabolic steroids.

Clearly, the physical and psychological risks of taking steroids are quite serious. But the negative consequences of taking these substances involve more than a user's health. Because steroids are illegal, buying and using them can also affect a person's personal freedom and liberty.

MAJOR LEAGUE BASEBALL COMMISSIONER BUD SELIG SPEAKS WITH U.S. SENATOR GEORGE ALLEN BEFORE TESTIFYING IN FRONT OF THE SENATE COMMERCE, SCIENCE AND TRANSPORTATION COMMITTEE ABOUT STEROID USE IN SPORTS IN WASHINGTON ON MARCH 10, 2004. SELIG TOLD THE PANEL THAT MAJOR LEAGUE BASEBALL NEEDS A STRINGENT STEROID TESTING POLICY SIMILAR TO THE ONE USED IN THE MINOR LEAGUES.

4 The Law and Steroids

MARKETING, SELLING, OR buying anabolic steroids is illegal. In 1988 Congress passed the Anti-Drug Abuse Act, which made distributing and possessing anabolic steroids for nonmedical uses a federal crime. In 1990 Congress passed an even more stringent law: the Anabolic Steroid Control Act. This act put the Drug Enforcement Administration (DEA) in charge of regulating and controlling anabolic steroids.

Under this law, anyone found making, selling, or possessing steroids faces up to five years in federal prison and a fine of up to $250,000 for his or her first offense and up to ten years in federal prison and a fine of up to $500,000 for a second offense.

Despite these harsh penalties, the underground sale of these banned substances remains a multi-billion-dollar industry today. The drugs that are sold are neither regulated nor tested, as prescription drugs are, which makes them even more dangerous to those who use and abuse them.

In addition, because of the illegality of anabolic steroids and because of the unfair physical advan-

National and International Sports Organizations that Ban Steroids

United States and International Olympic committees

American College of Sports Medicine

National Football League

U.S. Powerlifting Federation

National Collegiate Athletic Association

International Federation of Bodybuilders

tage those athletes who take these substances have over those who don't, drug testing by schools, workplaces, and the government is now widespread. Some people argue that random drug testing is an invasion of privacy. Others believe it is a necessary evil to protect the integrity of athletic programs and the athletes themselves.

The Steroid Black Market

Because possessing steroids without a prescription is illegal in the United States, a black market, which is the trade of illegal goods in violation of the law, has developed over the past twenty years or so. Secret laboratories in the United States and licensed plants outside the country produce the drugs. Drug traffickers then sell the drugs to individuals. About 20 percent of steroid users get their drugs from health professionals.

The DEA works to track down the sale and purchase of steroids in the United States and other countries. Charles E. Yesalis and Virginia Cowart have documented some of the DEA's successful efforts. According to Yesalis and Cowart, during the 1990s the DEA:

- seized more than two million dosage units of legitimate and counterfeit steroids in Detroit, Michigan;

- investigated a former Mr. Universe, who was then charged in a fourteen-count indictment with being the East Coast distributor for an international trafficker in steroids;

- conducted more than 350 anabolic steroid investigations between 1991 and 1995 alone, resulting in more than four hundred arrests and two hundred convictions.

In Mexican pharmacies, steroids can be purchased as over-the-counter drugs. The prices are about 40 percent lower than if purchased in the United States with a doctor's prescription. According to experts, many Americans travel to Mexico to buy the drugs and then smuggle them across the U.S.-Mexico border.

The criminalization of steroids has given rise to new problems. Once these drugs became contraband, many athletes bought black market anabolic steroids that were combined with other drugs or intended solely for veterinary use. Furthermore, because it is illegal to prescribe steroids for promoting muscle growth unless a patient is physically ill, physicians are unable to provide steroid users with responsible, professionally informed guidance.

Drug Testing for Steroids

Testing of human urine for the presence of per-formance-enhancing substances began in the 1950s. At that time, the Italian soccer and cycling federations requested lab tests of the athletes for the presence of stimulants. Then, after the 1960 Summer Olympics, the Italian National Olympic Committee joined forces with the sports federation

THE AUSTRALIAN GOVERNMENT ANALYTICAL LABORATORIES IN SYDNEY, AUSTRALIA WAS RESPONSIBLE FOR ANALYZING ATHLETE URINE SAMPLES DURING THE 2000 SYDNEY OLYMPIC GAMES.

to set up another drug-testing lab in Rome. Other European countries, including France, Austria, and Germany, followed suit and began testing their own athletes. Today, drug testing for these substances is common not only among sports organizations but also in high schools and colleges that seek to prevent their amateur athletes from abusing performance-enhancing drugs.

How Do They Test for Steroids?

The most common form of testing for steroids is a urine test. The first step in such a test involves obtaining a urine sample from the person being tested. A trained technician then subjects the urine to testing in a special machine called a gas chromatograph. The machine first separates the components of the urine sample and then heats them, changing the components into gases. The gases then pass through a machine called a spectrometer, which identifies the substances within the gases. A positive test means steroids are present. In some cases doctors will choose to take a blood sample from the person being tested. Testing the blood results in a more accurate measure of steroids in the body, but it requires a more expensive and complicated method. Steroids may remain detectable in the body anywhere from one week to one year after use.

Samantha, a thirteen-year-old competitor in gymnastics, admits that she's heard about other girls using steroids to try to get stronger, but she and her friends stay far away from those drugs. "We don't get tested now, but we will get tested when we get to high school. I, for one, don't want to count on my success depending on using drugs that could get me thrown off the team, never mind hurt my body. It's just not worth it."

And never mind testing, says Samantha. "It's pretty easy to tell when people are using steroids, even without a test. People get moody and their skin breaks out, and they never seem to get tired." Indeed, even at her young age, Samantha thinks she knows a steroid abuser when she sees one.

Why Test for Steroids?

The main reason for drug testing is deterrence, or preventing criminal behavior through fear of punishment. However, at this time the only people who are tested for steroids are athletes, either in schools or in certain professional or amateur organizations. Therefore, only athletes will be deterred from using due to fear of being caught through drug testing. According to some studies though, about 30 to 40 percent of anabolic steroid users in high school and college do not compete in competitive sports. Instead, they use them to enhance their appearance, increase their self-confidence, or as part of a pattern of other risk-taking behavior. For this reason and others, many question whether the deterrence effect of drug testing is a solution to the steroid abuse problem in the United States.

Is Drug Testing Constitutional?

There is also controversy about whether or not drug testing, for steroids or other drugs, is constitutional. The Fourth Amendment of the United States Constitution ensures "the right of the people to be secure in their persons, houses, papers, and effects against unreasonable searches and seizures. . . ." In order to protect that right, police officers and other government officials must have a warrant from a judge before they can require a citizen to open their homes or provide such physical evidence as urine or hair samples as evidence. In three cases the U.S. Supreme Court has considered whether drug testing without a warrant is an unreasonable search and seizure, which infringes on the right of privacy under the Fourth Amendment.

In *Treasury Employees* v. *Von Raab* (1989), for instance, the Court considered whether random drug-testing of certain United States Customs Service employees was constitutional. In that case, the Customs Service wanted to test employees who would be involved in drug interdiction or handling firearms. According to the Supreme Court, drug testing under those circumstances was reasonable because the expectation of privacy held by the Customs Service employees was outweighed by compelling government interests.

Using the same balancing test in *Skinner* v. *Railway Labor Executives Association* (1989), the Supreme Court ruled that random drug-testing of certain railway employees was constitutional. The interest in protecting passengers and other employees from the dangers posed by an employee operating a train far outweighed the right of the employee to be free from having to take a drug test.

SEVENTEEN-YEAR-OLD ROMANIAN GYMNAST ANDREEA RADUCAN PERFORMS AT THE 2000 SYDNEY OLYMPIC GAMES. RADUCAN WON THE GOLD MEDAL FOR WOMEN'S ALL-AROUND, THEN LOST THE TITLE WHEN TESTS REVEALED THAT COLD TABLETS SHE HAD TAKEN PRIOR TO THE COMPETITION CONTAINED A BANNED SUBSTANCE.

In *Vernonia School District No. 471 v. Acton* (1995), the Supreme Court directly addressed high school and college athletics. In that case the Court found that a school district's random drug-testing of athletes was constitutional under the Fourth Amendment. Their reasoning in this case was primarily twofold: First, the seriousness of the safety issues surrounding the use of illicit drugs made the search of the students reasonable and outweighed any privacy rights of the students. Second, random testing does not discriminate against any individual student forced to take the test.

Should Steroids Be Legalized?

Some people have suggested that illicit drugs of all kinds, including steroids, should be legalized. They suggest this idea for several reasons. Legalizing drugs would eliminate the very high costs spent by the government to enforce the laws against the trafficking and sale of the substances. Costs include those incurred by police officers to investigate and arrest offenders, by the criminal justice system that prosecutes the offenders, and by the prison system that must incarcerate those convicted of drug offenses.

Those in favor of legalizing drugs also believe that if drugs like steroids were legal, then there would be more control over both the quality of the substances used and the way in which people use them. The FDA is the government agency that regulates prescription drugs and acts to monitor vitamins, minerals, and other similar legal substances. If steroids were legal, the FDA would also control their manufacture, sale, and safety. Without such oversight by a federal agency, people who take steroids without a prescription and without being under a doctor's care are not exactly sure of what they are putting into their bodies. In fact, some of the steroids sold on the black market are actually veterinary drugs used to treat animals. Also, if steroids were legal, then people who wanted to use them could take them under a doctor's care. Such medical monitoring perhaps would help users avoid some of the serious side effects that result from taking high doses of these drugs.

The arguments against legalizing steroids are equally strong. Critics say that no matter how closely doctors and government agencies monitor steroid use, these drugs still pose serious health risks to those who take them. And, perhaps most importantly, taking steroids to improve athletic performance would remain a way of gaining an advantage—an unfair advantage, opponents of legalized steroids claim—over athletes who choose not to risk their health to build muscle "the easy way." Finally, some opponents argue that legalizing steroids would only encourage those with perfectly normal bodies to strive to alter their physiques at the risk of endangering their health.

WORKING OUT WITH A TRAINER IS ONE OF THE HEALTHY WAYS TO BUILD MUSCLE.

5 Prevention, Treatment, and Healthy Fitness

"ALL I CARED ABOUT was winning, winning, winning..." former professional football player Lyle Alzado told a reporter for *Sports Illustrated* in 1991. Alzado admitted to taking steroids throughout his career and even after he retired—right up until his death in 1992. He also admitted knowing almost all along that taking steroids was doing him more harm than good, physically and psychologically.

"I started taking anabolic steroids in 1969 and I never stopped," he said. "Now I'm sick, and I'm scared.... My strength isn't my strength anymore.... If you're on steroids or human growth hormone, stop. I should have." Just a year after giving this interview, Lyle Alzado was dead—succumbing to brain cancer, an illness he attributed at least in part to his use of steroids. Ceasing the use of steroids after even a short time may be difficult. Many people need physical and emotional support to do so.

Treating Steroid Abuse

People decide to use steroids for a number of reasons. Most do so in an attempt to enhance their athletic ability because they play (or want to play) an amateur or professional organized sport. Others take steroids to alter their personalities, hoping to become more aggressive or less shy. Still others are continuing a pattern of drug abuse or other risk-taking behavior.

Many young men and young women take steroids in an attempt to improve a low self-image about their bodies. In such people steroid abuse may accompany or replace an eating disorder, such as bulimia or anorexia nervosa. Scientists are still unsure about what causes some people to lose their appetite altogether, as with anorexia nervosa, or to eat and purge, as with bulimia; but experts agree that media images of impossibly thin movie actresses and models and well-toned bodybuilders may trigger, or at least fuel, these conditions.

Although it is mostly women who suffer from eating disorders, about 10 percent of people with bulimia or anorexia are men. In addition, a growing body of evidence suggests that men may be vulnerable to a newly identified condition called muscle dysphoria. Someone who has muscle dysphoria obsesses about lacking muscle definition and mass, even if they have muscular bodies. As Katherine A. Beals PhD, RD, told *Health & Fitness Journal* in March/April 2003, "Millions of boys and men today harbor a secret obsession about their looks and are endangering their health by engaging in excessive exercise, binging and purging rituals, steroid abuse, and overuse of nutritional and dietary [products]."

Treatment for steroid abuse consists primarily of getting an abuser to stop taking the drugs. Doing so involves addressing the reasons that the abuser started using steroids in the first place, with the help of a counselor or psychologist. Someone who takes steroids because he or she wants to increase muscle size may require a different kind of psychological support than someone who takes them because he or she has a body image disorder.

Another goal when it comes to treating steroid addiction is to minimize the physical and psychological withdrawal symptoms, which can include any of the following:

Depression
Headaches
Insomnia
Nausea
Cravings for steroids
Sweating
Weight loss
Shrinking muscles
Loss of energy

Some of the symptoms listed—specifically depression, headaches, nausea, and particularly cravings for more of the same substance—are also common to those suffered by people who stop taking other drugs, such as cocaine and heroin. They occur because the body and mind have become dependent upon—even addicted to—the effects of the steroids to feel "normal." This leads us to an important question—are steroids really addictive?

Are Steroids Addictive?

According to *Merriam-Webster's Collegiate Dictionary,* the definition of *addiction* is a "compulsive need for and use of a habit-forming substance (as heroin, nicotine, or alcohol) characterized by tolerance and by well-defined physiological symptoms upon withdrawal, broadly, persistent compulsive use of a substance known by the user to be harmful." When people are addicted to an illicit drug, stopping the use of that drug causes side effects, called withdrawal symptoms, and some of them are severe. Whether or not steroids are addictive in the same way as other drugs, such as heroin and cocaine, remains a subject of debate. However, more and more studies indicate that many of those who use steroids may become physically and psychologically addicted to them. That means they will suffer from withdrawal symptoms—and cravings for the drug to avoid those symptoms—when they stop taking them.

Jason, a sixteen-year-old member of his high school's wrestling team, tapered off using steroids the summer before his junior year, when his high school announced that it would start random testing. Jason remarked,

Even though I did it "right" by tapering off, I still felt pretty bad for a while. I felt depressed and edgy at the same time. I had headaches, too. I didn't give in, but I did keep thinking that if I just took a little more of the steroids, then I'd feel better. I threw out all the stuff I had, but it didn't stop me from wanting it all the time. But after the headaches went away, and my moods were more even, I knew I wasn't going to use again.

In a study published in a 1991 *British Journal of Addiction,* scientists found that the most frequently reported withdrawal symptoms were cravings for steroids (52 percent), fatigue (43 percent), depressed mood (41 percent), restlessness (29 percent), no appetite (24 percent), difficulty in falling asleep (20 percent), decreased interest in sex (20 percent), and headaches (20 percent).

How to Break Free

So how does a person who becomes dependent on steroids break free? The answer to that question remains complicated. Unfortunately, few studies of treatments for anabolic steroid abuse have been conducted so far, and what we know is based largely on the experiences of a small number of physicians who have worked with patients undergoing steroid withdrawal. According to the National Institute on Drug Abuse, these physicians have found that supportive therapy through a family physician or psychologist can help the user cope with the physical and emotional effects and side effects of steroid withdrawal. This doctor will educate the abuser about what to expect during withdrawal and help him or her through the process.

If symptoms are severe or prolonged, the doctor may suggest medication or even hospitalization. Some medications that have been used for treating steroid withdrawal restore the hormonal system,

CARDIOVASCULAR EXERCISE, SUCH AS RUNNING, IS AN IMPORTANT PART OF ANY
FITNESS PROGRAM.

CALISTHENICS ARE MUSCLE-BUILDING EXERCISES PERFORMED WITHOUT ANY APPARATUS.

which has been disrupted by the steroid abuse. Other medications target specific withdrawal symptoms. If the person is feeling depressed, for example, a doctor might prescribe an antidepressant. If the abuser suffers from headaches, aspirin or ibuprofen will help minimize the pain.

Some patients require assistance beyond simple treatment of withdrawal symptoms and are treated with psychological therapy. Support groups like Al-Anon and Narcotics Anonymous can also help. Other sources of help and support include:

- teachers and school counselors
- coaches and athletic directors
- local mental health agencies
- local drug abuse centers

Building Muscles the Healthy Way
Instead of risking mental and physical health by taking steroids, muscle strength and endurance can be built through diet and exercise. Building muscles requires applying resistance—weight—to normal body motion. This resistance makes muscles contract at an increased tension, which causes them to grow and become stronger.

You can add resistance in two ways: through the weight of your own body by doing exercises called calisthenics or by using handheld weights or weight machines. Weight training will build muscle more quickly than calisthenics. Weights provide more resistance to make muscles work harder. Therefore the muscles will grow and become stronger more quickly.

Because the techniques of calisthenics and weight training are very precise and if not performed correctly can lead to injury, a visit to the local gym or YMCA for professional instruction is key. Indeed, safety is a prime issue when it comes to weight training, especially for young people and teens. According to the U.S. Consumer Product Safety Commission, 35 percent of the estimated 60,000 injuries linked to weight-lifting equipment in 1998 involved people ages fifteen to twenty-four, while children ages five to fourteen were involved in 12 percent of such accidents. However, properly supervised training using light weights in a controlled manner does not pose a danger to young people. Lifting weights that are too heavy in a jerky motion, like well-trained power lifters do poses "a significant risk of injury" for teens, the American Academy of Pediatrics (AAP) says.

In addition to exercising to build muscle, a balanced diet is necessary to provide a growing body with all the nutrition it needs. Getting all the essential vitamins and minerals is important for any teen, but even more crucial for anyone involved in weight training or other fitness or athletic programs.

What's a Good Routine?

Before getting started on a weight-training plan, students should talk to a coach at their school, a fitness trainer at a local gym or YMCA, and/or read up on proper techniques at the local library. Safety, more than quick results, should remain the most important factor in choosing and participating in a fitness program.

Set realistic goals, both short-term and long-term. Weight training toward competing in—and winning—bodybuilding competitions in three weeks is unrealistic. It is best to work with a coach or a trainer to set realistic goals.

"No pain, no gain" is a myth. Performed improperly, any kind of exercise can cause serious injury. Pain is a warning sign, a message from the body that something is wrong and needs attention. At the very least, if exercise causes pain or leads to muscle ache, a person is likely to end up discouraged rather than excited and motivated. One should feel challenged by the effort, but there should never be pain of any kind.

Choose enjoyable activities. If the goal is to build muscle, then some type of weight training is necessary. But weight training alone can lead to boredom and dissatisfaction. Incorporating a variety of exercises into one's life keeps it interesting. Running will help build stamina and leg muscle; yoga keeps

Stacy, now a twenty-two-year-old college graduate, remembers when she quit steroids during her first year of college, after using them to try to control her weight and reshape her body during high school.

At first, it was really hard. I had to work harder to keep my shape. But then I started playing tennis—I'd never been athletic at all, even though I used steroids!—and found that although I would never be mistaken for a model, I felt so much better about myself, stronger even, prettier even. My female shape began to come back, and I felt better physically. It sounds like a cliche´ but regular exercise and a good diet does more for you all around than any drug.

muscles flexible and lithe; swimming calms the mind as it strengthens the arms.

A weight routine should train the entire body. Weight-training experts suggest working the mid-section first, followed by chest, back, shoulders, biceps, triceps, and legs. Working with a trainer is the best way to maintain a workout schedule and to choose the most beneficial exercises.

• Make a commitment. It takes at least six weeks for a new behavior to become a habit. If one is serious about building muscle, getting stronger, and having fun by competing or participating in high school athletics, he or she needs to hang in there and stick to a set schedule. After a while, life will not seem complete without regular exercise.

• Safety first. Again, nothing will shut down a fitness program faster than an injury, even a minor one. Weight training with machines or free weights should be done with a trained professional, who can help set up a program that is both safe and effective. Experts agree that teens should not try to use the maximum amount of weight they are capable of lifting until they are fully mature.

• Eat well. Protein is an important compo-
nent of every person's diet, especially those
involved in a weight-training program.
Protein helps to form and build muscle tissue
and should make up about 10 to 15 percent
of one's daily diet. The human body needs a
variety of foods to stay healthy. Carbohydrates,
such as those in whole grain breads and
pasta, provide energy. Fruits and vegetables
contain important vitamins and minerals the
body cannot thrive without. A school dieti-
tian can answer any questions about proper
nutrition, and there are plenty of books
about healthy nutrition at the school library.

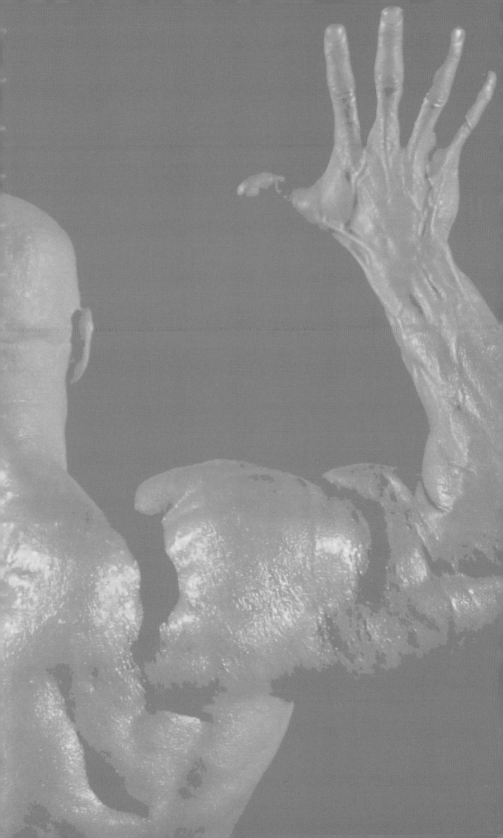

GLOSSARY

aerobic exercise: Physical exercise that relies on the intake of oxygen for energy production.

addiction: Physical and psychological dependence on a substance or behavior; a chronic, relapsing disease characterized by compulsive drug-seeking and abuse and by long-lasting chemical changes in the brain.

anabolic effects: Drug-induced growth or thickening of the body's non-reproductive tract tissues, including skeletal muscle, bones, the larynx, and vocal cords, and decrease in body fat.

androgenic effects: A drug's effects upon the growth of the male reproductive tract and the development of male secondary sexual characteristics.

black market: The illegal buying and selling of drugs and other substances.

carbohydrates: A class of food that includes sugars and starches; the main source of energy utilized by humans.

cardiovascular system: The heart together with the two networks of vessels: arteries and veins. Transports nutrients and oxygen to the tissues and removes waste products.

cholesterol: A fatlike substance found in the brain, nerves, liver, blood, and bile. Synthesized in the liver, cholesterol is essential to a number of bodily functions. Excess cholesterol that has been through the process of oxidization contributes to cardiovascular disease.

corticosteroids: Synthetic steroids used to treat certain diseases.

cycle: The eight-to-twelve-week period when steroids are used.

endocrine system: The system of glands and other structures that secrete hormones into the bloodstream, including the thyroid, adrenal, pituitary, pineal, and pancreas.

estrogen: A group of female hormones responsible for the development of secondary sex traits and aspects of reproduction. Produced in the ovaries, adrenal glands, testicles, and in fat tissue.

growth hormone: A hormone secreted by the pituitary gland and is instrumental in regulating growth. It is controlled by the central nervous system, and the body releases it in bursts, especially during sleep.

hormone: A chemical produced by the endocrine glands or tissue that, when secreted into body fluids, has a specific effect on other organs and processes. Hormones often are referred to as "chemical messengers" and they influence such diverse activities as growth, sexual development, metabolism, and sleep cycles. Hormones also are instrumental in maintaining the proper internal chemical and fluid balance.

hypogondasim: A condition that exists when a man's body fails to produce enough testerone for normal growth, development, and sexual function.

immune system: The system that wards off infection and responds to illness.

insomnia: A chronic inability to sleep or to remain asleep at night. Caused by a variety of factors, including diet and exercise, drug use, and hormonal imbalances.

metabolism: The sum of all chemical processes that take place in the body essential to convert food to the energy needed to sustain life.

musculoskeletal system: The muscles, bones, tendons, and ligaments.

osteoporosis: A loss of bone density that occurs as a result of calcium and magnesium imbalances, along with lack of exercise, in middle to old age. Osteoporosis causes increased porousness and brittleness in the bones.

progesterone: A hormone secreted by the adrenals and ovaries the levels of which rise during the second phase of the menstrual cycle.

roid rage: A slang term for the uncontrolled anger, frustration, and/or combativeness that often result from the use of anabolic steroids.

serotonin: A naturally-occurring chemical derived from the amino acid tryptophan.

steroid: Any of a large number of hormonal substances with the same basic chemical structure as those produced in the adrenal cortex and gonads.

stress: Any factor—physical or emotional—that has an effect on the body.

testosterone: A naturally-occurring hormone responsible for the development of male sex characteristics.

vitamin: Any of a group of substances required by the body for healthy growth and development, as well as cell repair.

withdrawal: Symptoms that occur after chronic use of a drug is stopped or reduced.

FURTHER INFORMATION

Books

Clayton, Lawrence and Rosen Group Staff. *Steroids.* New York: Rosen Publishing Group, 1999.

Kuhn, Cynthia, Scott Swartzwelder, and Wilkie Wilson. *Just Say Know: Talking with Kids about Drugs and Alcohol.* New York: W. W. Norton & Company, 2002.

Lukas, Scott E. Ph.D. *Steroids.* Berkeley Heights, NJ: Enslow Publishers, 1994.

Monroe, Judy. *Steroid Drug Dangers.* Berkeley Heights, NJ: Enslow Publishers, 1999.

Peck, Rodney G. *Drugs and Sports.* New York: Rosen Publishing Group, 1997.

Wright, James. *Anabolic Steroids: Altered States.* Indianapolis, IN: Masters Press, 1994.

Yesais, Charles E. and Virginia S. Cowart. *The Steroids Game: An expert's inside look at anabolic steroid use in sports.* Champaign, IL: Human Kinetics, 1998.

Medical Journals

Blue, J. G. and J. A. Lambardo. 1999. "Steroids and steroid-like compounds." *Clinics in Sports Medicine* 18(3):667–668.

Brower K. J. , G. A. Eliopulos, F. C. Blow, D. H. Catlin, and T. P. Beresford 1990. "Evidence for physical and psychological dependence on anabolic androgenic steroids in eight weight lifters." *American Journal of Psychiatry* 147(4):510–512.

Goldberg, L. et. al. 2000. "The ATLAS program: Preventing drug use and promoting healthy behaviors." *Archives of Pediatrics and Adolescent Medicine* 154:332–38.

Gruber, A .J. and H. G. Pope, Jr. 2000. "Psychiatric and medical effects of anabolic-androgenic steroid use in women." *Psychotherapy and Psychosomatics* 69:19–26.

Hoberman, J. M. and C. E. Yesalis. 1995. "The history of synthetic testosterone." *Scientific American* 272(2):76–81.

Leder, B.Z. et al. 2000. "Oral androstenedione administration and serum testosterone concentrations in young men." *Journal of the American Medical Association* 283(6):779–782.

Middleman, A. B. et al. 1995. "High-risk behaviors among high school students in Massachusetts who use anabolic steroids." *Pediatrics* 96(2):268–272.

Pope, H. G., E. M. Kouri, and M. D. Hudson. 2000. "Effects of supraphysiologic doses of testosterone on mood and aggression in normal men." *Archives of General Psychiatry* 57(2):13–140.

Sullivan, M. L., C. M. Martinez, P. Gennis, and E. J. Gallagher. 1998. "The cardiac toxicity of anabolic steroids." *Progress in Cardiovascular Diseases* 41(1):1–15.

Zarpette, G. 1998. "Andro angst." *Scientific American* 279(6):22–26.

Web Sites

Al-Anon/Alateen

www.al-anon.org

According to its Web site, Al-Anon and its teen division, Alateen, are designed "to help families and friends of alcoholics recover from the effects of living with the problem drinking of a relative or friend. Similarly, Alateen is our recovery program for young people. Alateen groups are sponsored by Al-Anon members." Its program of recovery is adapted from Alcoholics Anonymous and is based upon the Twelve Steps, Twelve Traditions, and Twelve Concepts of Service. Since many steroid abusers also abuse alcohol and other drugs, this site, and the Alateen program, may help those abusers address their problem.

National Center on Addiction and Substance Abuse

www.casacolumbia.org

Columbia University in New York City funds an organization that focuses on drug abuse and its treatment. Its Web site offers lots of information directed specifically at teen, and provides lists of links to other drug-related Web sites.

Mayo Clinic
www.mayohealth.org
One of the most renowned medical centers in the world, the Mayo Clinic also has a Web site where you can find information not only about almost every condition and disease known to mankind but also about steroids and their effects and side effects. The clinic Web site also offers a page all about building muscle naturally through diet and exercise.

Partnership for a Drug Free America
www.drugfreeameria.org
This nonprofit, private organization provides information about steroids and other substances on its Web site. It offers pages just for parents as well as a kid-friendly question-and-answer page.

INDEX

ABOUT THE AUTHOR

Suzanne LeVert is the author of more than twenty-five young adult and adult nonfiction titles. She specializes in health and medical subjects as well as the social sciences. For Marshall Cavendish's Celebrate the States series, Ms. LeVert contributed *Massachusetts* and *Louisiana*. Born in Natick, Massachusetts, Ms. LeVert now practices law in New Orleans, Louisiana, where she comes face to face with the legal and social problems caused by illegal drug addiction and trafficking.